NATURAL HOME

Copyright © 2010 Laura Ashley Limited

First published in 2010 by Blue Sky Books Ltd
2nd Floor, Berkeley Square House, Berkeley Square, London W1J 6BD
www.blueskybooks.co.uk

British Cataloguing-in-Publication Data:
A catalogue record of this book is available from the British Library.

ISBN 978-1-907309-04-5

Designed by Spirit Design Consultants, London
www.spirit-design.com

Printed and bound in China through Printworks Int. Ltd.

CONTENTS

INTRODUCTION

Our home is our haven, it is where we relax.

The Natural Home is a lovely, simple introduction into living
more in tune with nature. From furnishings and accessories
that blend effortlessly, to the simple, easy ways we can
look after our home.

There are many natural elements that make up where we live,
the furniture in our living room, the plants on our coffee table
and the scents and fragrances that uplift us. Not forgetting
nature's simple pleasures like fresh air and glorious daylight.

This simple book celebrates nature in our life
and the joy of keeping things simple.

ACCESSORIES

A home filled with natural objects not only looks good, it's good for our well-being. Having natural things around us makes can make us feel energised and healthy.

Accessories are the easiest way of bringing the feeling of the outdoors into our home. Natural elements such as wood and stone and fabrics such as cotton and linen are simple and beautiful.

Terracotta pots add warmth and earthiness to any room. They can be found in a variety of shapes and sizes and look just as good dressing a living room windowsill, as they do a kitchen table.

Look to the outdoors for beautiful, natural accessories,
such as shells, wood pieces and pebbles. They add a unique
feature to your home and a really natural feel to any room.

※

Fresh fruit makes a beautiful display.
Apples look particularly beautiful in a large wooden bowl.

※

Candles are a clean and simple way to decorate any room.
They look attractive and instantly refresh and
scent a room when lit.

※

The fireplace is the heart of the home and looks beautiful dressed simply with natural accessories. A favourite plant, some handpicked flowers or a pine mirror all work beautifully to make this the centrepiece of your room.

✳

Logs, wood and twigs are wonderful in a fireplace, creating a decorative feature to a room. Try adding some sprigs of rosemary and lavender for extra scent and colour.

✳

Wood has a warm and inviting feel to it. A wooden bowl or ornament has a simple, natural beauty and looks attractive displayed on a mantelpiece against a neutral coloured wall.

✳

Mirrors are not only decorative, they can help
add more light to a room, perfect for making
the space feel bright and airy.

Candlestick holders, in an antique finish or glass, add
a touch of natural style to a room. They are simple
but very effective. A white antique finish looks
beautiful in a living room or bedroom.

Simple white pots are perfect for displaying plants,
pot pourri and flowers. They are clean and simple and
keep the focus on the object.

COLOUR AND LIGHT

Natural daylight is an instant mood lifter and enhances the home. Make the most of the daylight by dressing windows in voile, muslin or other light fabrics that brighten your home.

Fresh air is another of nature's best tonics. It may sound simple, but letting fresh air flow through the house adds instant freshness to the whole home.

Neutral colours are perfect for creating the natural feel.
Beige, oatmeal and pale brown colours, together with creams
and soft whites, all remind us of nature's soothing colours.

�֎

Add to the feeling by using soft greens, pale blues and
soothing yellows to enhance the feeling of nature.

✷

Soft and gentle colours reflect light, making your space
look bright and airy.

✷

Natural daylight is the greatest asset of the natural home. Dressing windows in soft coloured fabrics and using tie-backs is another very effective way of letting more light into your home, adding to the sense of space and airiness in a room.

Lighting can set the tone and feel of a room. There are a variety of light bulbs available. Natural daylight bulbs are particularly effective in an area used to work and read.

Lampshades can add to the organic feel of a home. Try a wicker or paper shade to create a soft, relaxed feel.

FABRICS AND FURNISHINGS

A linen cupboard is not only ideal for keeping all
your sheets, pillowcases and bed linen beautifully
organised, it can also be a feature in itself,
perfectly suited to a landing or guest room.

Care for your duvet by shaking it and fluffing it every
morning and wherever possible airing it outside.

Make your own linen spray using a few drops of
lavender essence and water. It smells wonderful
and keeps bedding lovely and fresh.

Cushions in a variety of natural fabrics and textures are the
perfect way to add a casual and easy feel to the home.

�֍

Throws are very versatile and can lift a chair or sofa.
A throw in heavy cotton or wool looks wonderful
on a light coloured sofa or leather chair.

✷

Curtains can be a strong focal point in any room.
A beautiful pair of neutral coloured cotton or
jacquard curtains can frame a window beautifully
and blend effortlessly with the outdoors.

✷

Switch your curtains around to opposite ends of the window every time you take them down for washing or cleaning, so that they will retain their colour more evenly.

✳

Natural fabrics tend to look better and create an easy, relaxed style that man made fabrics cannot achieve.

✳

Linen, cotton and jacquards are beautiful to the feel and tend to drape better, which gives them a lovely natural touch around the home.

✳

Rugs are a simple way to add style and individuality to a room and they work well on a wooden or stone floor. They can be cared for by beating over a washing line. Leave them in the fresh air for a wonderful, outdoors smell.

✽

Runners in heavy cotton are durable, easy to care for and perfect for frequently used areas of the home such as hallways and doorways. They can help protect natural floors such as wood and slate.

✽

For a quick, easy rug deodoriser, sprinkle baking powder on carpets before vacuuming and add some crushed lavender for fragrance.

✽

Store blankets, covers and quilts in vacuum bags.
The bags are perfect for saving space and protect
against damp, dust and mildew.

※

A well organised home has many benefits; apart
from finding items easily, there is a sense of satisfaction
in knowing everything has a place. With so many attractive,
natural storage options in wood, rattan, fabric and paper,
storage can look good and be practical too.

※

Wicker baskets are perfect for storing all those
loose bits and bobs. They look good in most rooms
and have a lovely, natural feel to them.

※

FLOWERS AND PLANTS

To enhance a simple flower arrangement, try using
a few sprigs of fresh herbs. Greenery such as mint, thyme
and rosemary is a lovely way of adding extra colour,
as well as creating a wonderful fragrance.

※

A kitchen table always looks good with a focal point
and flowers are usually the first choice. Try displaying them
in different ways other than a vase. A vintage teapot or
glass bowl is a lovely alternative.

※

A vase filled with flowers from the garden is a simple
but very effective centerpiece.

※

Keep flowers fresh for as long as possible by changing
the water and cutting off a small piece of the stems
every day. If the stems are hard and woody, like rose stems,
it is best to crush them at the ends, which encourages
them to absorb water. If you can't change the water every
day, a piece of charcoal or a copper coin in the water
will help your flowers last longer.

Tulips are simple, pretty and look lovely in a plain
glass vase. To make them last longer, make a line
of small holes down the entire length of their stems.

Fresh flowers are a must for any home. Flowers such as jasmine, sweat peas, narcissi and hyacinths are wonderfully fragrant and make a beautiful display in any room of the house.

�֍

House plants are a very simple of way of giving a room an instant lift. They add life and colour to any room and look stylish, as well as natural.

✷

Leafy plants are a very effective way of purifying the air, making where you live not only more attractive but healthier.

✷

FRAGRANCE

For a simple, but natural smelling room fragrance,
just light a candle. Try a delicious and warming
orange blossom scent to lift the room instantly.

To create a special scent around the home mix some
fresh rosemary, lavender and eucalyptus in a bowl. Try adding
some chopped basil too. The smell is wonderfully inviting.

If you are planning to be away for a week or so, place
a bowl of rosemary and lavender in the hall. The scent
lasts seven days and will keep the house smelling
good for your return.

A glass bowl of coffee beans is perfect for absorbing smells
like cigar smoke and leaves your home smelling delicious too.

※

Throw rosemary twigs and lavender onto a log fire.
The smell is glorious.

※

The rind from citrus fruits such as oranges, lemons,
limes and grapefruits make a wonderful, uplifting pot pourri.
Leave them in a glass bowl to scent a room.

※

Warm water is an excellent carrier for fragrances.
Add a few drops of scented essential oils to a bowl
of water and place in a favourite room of the house.
It will keep the room smelling fragrant for hours.

In a centrally heated home put some eucalyptus
leaves in the humidifiers above the radiators.

Vanilla is a wonderfully uplifting fragrance,
try it as a room scent or a candle for
a beautifully relaxing aroma.

FURNITURE

The essence of the natural home is simple and uncluttered. One or two carefully selected items of furniture create a relaxed, yet stylish look. A maple dresser or light wood display cabinet capture the feel perfectly.

The natural tones and characteristics of wood are beautiful in themselves and a piece of carefully chosen pine or oak furniture can become a personal treasure.

A large pine mirror is a simple, yet stylish method of adding depth to a room.

A wooden dresser is perfect for displaying
your favourite pictures and trinkets. Oak
and old pine woods have mature, rich tones
and a beautiful grain which look good in any room.

Good furniture is the heart of the house and a soft,
comfy chair the soul. Chairs have a character all of
their own and are perfect for snuggling up in.

A polished wood floor adds style, texture and warmth
to a room and gives it a distinctive natural style.

Keep furniture pieces out of direct sunlight.

Look after wooden pieces by buffing up the wood
with wax polish, this will allow you to see its texture
and individual characteristics. Some woods may need
oiling to keep them looking their best.

Quality, solid wood furniture is one of the best
investments you'll ever make for your home.
Care for it correctly and it will serve you well.

Natural Home

When dusting your home, begin at the highest
point and work your way down to the floors.

※

To clean floors the natural way, add some
lavender essence to a bucket of hot water. This works
on all hard floors, not just wood but stone too. Your room
will smell good and the lavender essence acts as a
cleaning agent, so no need to add soap.

※

Look after lampshades by giving them a regular
light dusting, it will help keep them looking their best.

※

To care for mattresses, turn them regularly and
vacuum both sides. Use a mattress protector
to prolong its life and keep it clean.

Look after pillows by using protector slips underneath
the pillowcase. Always wash pillows, never dry clean them
and wash them individually in the machine, except foam
pillows, which should be sponged. Pillows should be hung
to dry and shaken now and then to fluff up their contents.

Spraying sheets and pillowcases with a water spray
will make them easier to iron.

Porcelain and enamel baths and washbasins will keep their shiny appearance longer if you rub them with coarse salt.

White vinegar and water makes the perfect window cleaner. Mix one part vinegar and three parts water. Clean windows and then dry with newspaper. For a simple mirror cleaning solution mix equal parts vinegar and water in a spray bottle.

Try not to wash windows or glass when the sun is on them or if they are warm. This causes the solution to dry too quickly creating unwanted streaks.

Leather is one of the most organic materials
you will find and fits with ease into the natural home.
A soft chocolate brown leather chair is perfect near
the fire in winter or welcoming in a study or den.
With its distinct, unique appearance, leather always
looks good and, not only that, it looks even
better with age.

Regular dusting is essential as it is very
important to keep leather pores free from
dust particles. Simply wipe your leather chair
or sofa with a soft cloth. This may seem like
a small task, but it goes a long way in the
longer term care of your leather.

Dusty radiators give off far less heat than clean ones do. Make sure yours are regularly dusted.

Carpets and curtains will last longer if they are professionally cleaned at least once a year and there are plenty of natural, professional, care options available.

Baking soda is a versatile, natural general cleaner. Dissolve 4 tablespoons of baking soda in 1 quart of warm water. The solution is ideal for regular, light cleaning of work surfaces and floors.

Once a year, give your wardrobe and drawers a thorough
clean and finish with a mixture of water and lavender.
It will not only keep them clean but is a good excuse
to clear out unwanted items.

Line drawers with pretty draw liners, or beautiful
wallpaper, they will help protect your favourite
possessions and brighten up a chest of drawers.

Mix a spray bottle of water and rose essence
and spray frequently into drawers and wardrobes.

Photography credits

David Brittain
Page: FC, 1, 2, 6, 8, 12, 15, 16, 19, 22, 24, 27, 35, 36, 38, 44, 47, 48, 53, 57

Lee Garland
Page: 11, 20, 32, 43, 50, 54, 58

Polly Wreford
Page: 28, 31, 40, 61

Special thanks to

Anna Ball, Christina Burdett,

Joseph Franks, Iain Hector,

Paul Hooper, David Woods,

Jenny Woods